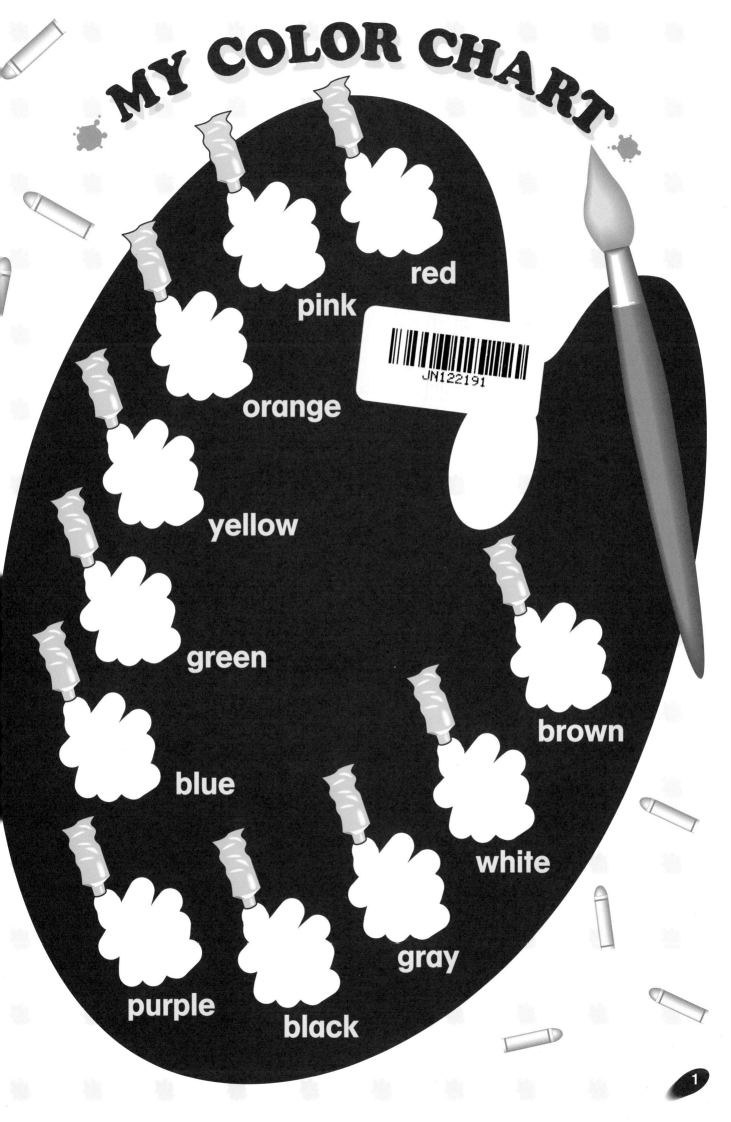

I'm finished!

This is me.

My name is

My eyes are

My hair is

This is my hand.

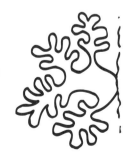

自分の手をなぞって目と口を描いて魚にしよう。
Trace your hand to make a fish.

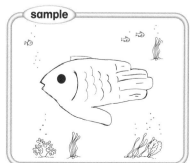

sample

I'm finished!

How many～?

| 1 | 2 | 3 | 4 | 5 | 6 | 7 | 8 | 9 | 10 |

I am ☐ years old.

自分の歳の数だけローソクを描きましょう。
Draw the number of candles that match your age.

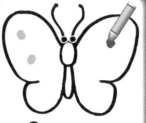

2 red dots
1 blue dot

1 red dot
3 blue dots

2 red dots
1 blue dot

3 red dots
2 blue dots

2 red dots
4 blue dots

2 red dots
1 blue dot

1 red dot
1 blue dot

2 red dots
2 blue dots

3 red dots
2 blue dots

2 red dots
5 blue dots

1 red dot
5 blue dots

1 red dot
2 blue dots

1 red dot
4 blue dots

7 red dots
2 blue dots

1 red dot
6 blue dots

4 red dots
1 blue dot

5 red dots
3 blue dots

7 red dots
6 blue dots

I'm finished!

My Family

My Family Tree

Where are you?

red

blue

green

pink

yellow

orange

purple

♡ Where is my mother? ♡

それぞれのお母さんをさがして、線でむすびましょう。自分のお母さんの顔をかいてみましょう。
Match the children and mothers and connect. Draw a picture of your mother.

I like  .

I'm wearing  ,

 ,

 ,

 ,

and

 today.

What color is No.1?

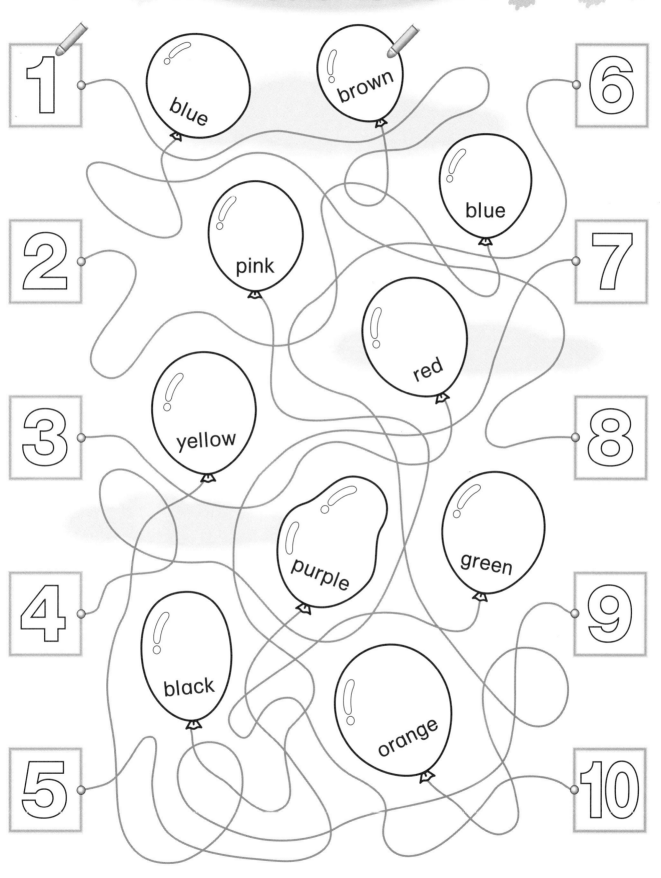

風船に色をぬって、同じ色を数字にもぬりましょう。
Color the balloons and the numbers.

green

yellow

blue

brown

white

pink

red

red

green

yellow

blue

yellow

I'm finished!

This is my foot.

blue eyes

green nose

red hair

black eyes

brown hair

red nose

  eyes   ○ nose    hair

Draw Humpty Dumpty.

1. Draw an egg.

2. Draw eyes.

3. Draw a nose.

4. Draw a mouth.

5. Draw clothes.

6. Draw legs.

7. Draw arms.

15

I'm finished!

H

A

N

K

Z

F

X

E

T

L

 # Find the animals.

□の中の絵をよく見てから隠し、どんな動物がいたか、⬤の中からさがして色をぬりましょう。
Look at the picture on the left then cover it. Guess which animals were in the picture and color.

I'm finished!

 # Draw a house.

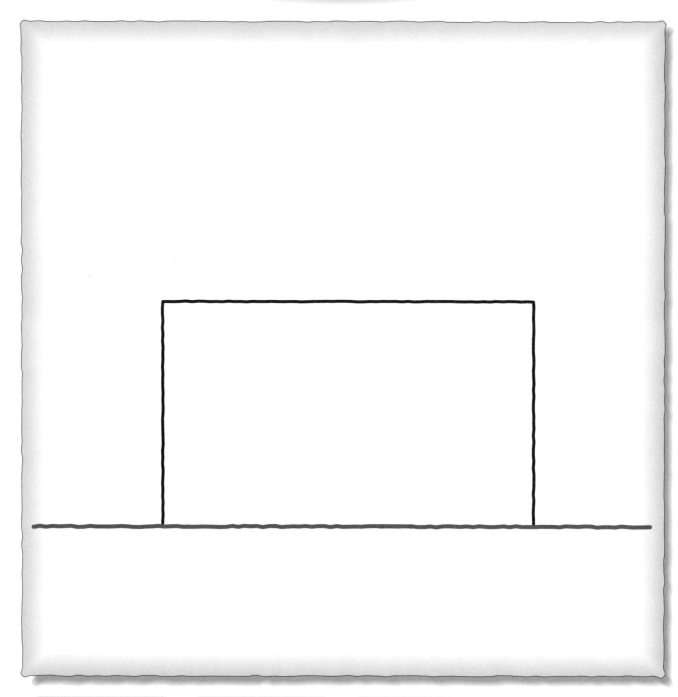

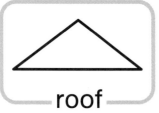
roof

chimney

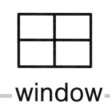
window

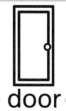
door

sun

cloud

tree

flower

grass

Which picture is missing?

( )   ( )   ( )   ( )

( )   ( )   ( )   ( )

( )   ( )   ( )   ( )

( )   ( )   ( )   ( )

( )   ( )   ( )   ( )

How many **big apples?**

How many **little apples?**

How many **big oranges?**

How many **little oranges?**

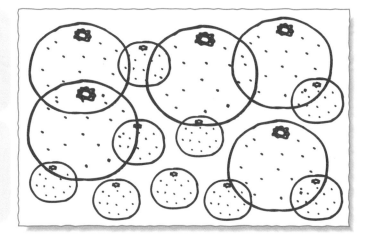

How many **big pineapples?**

How many **little pineapples?**

How many **big potatoes?**

How many **little potatoes?**

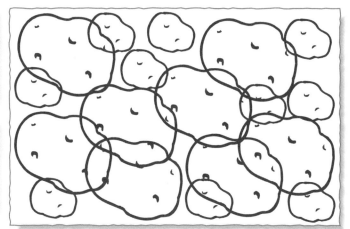

I'm finished!

pizza

salad

cake

apple pie

ice cream

hot dogs

pancakes

tomato juice

spaghetti

milk

orange juice

hamburgers

 I like "___". ············➤  red

 I don't like "___". ·······➤ blue

I'm finished!

 # Color the fruit!

five	four	three	two
four	five	two	three
three	one	five	two
five	four	six	two
one	six	three	five
six	three	five	two

one	two	three	four	five	six

I'm finished!

Maze

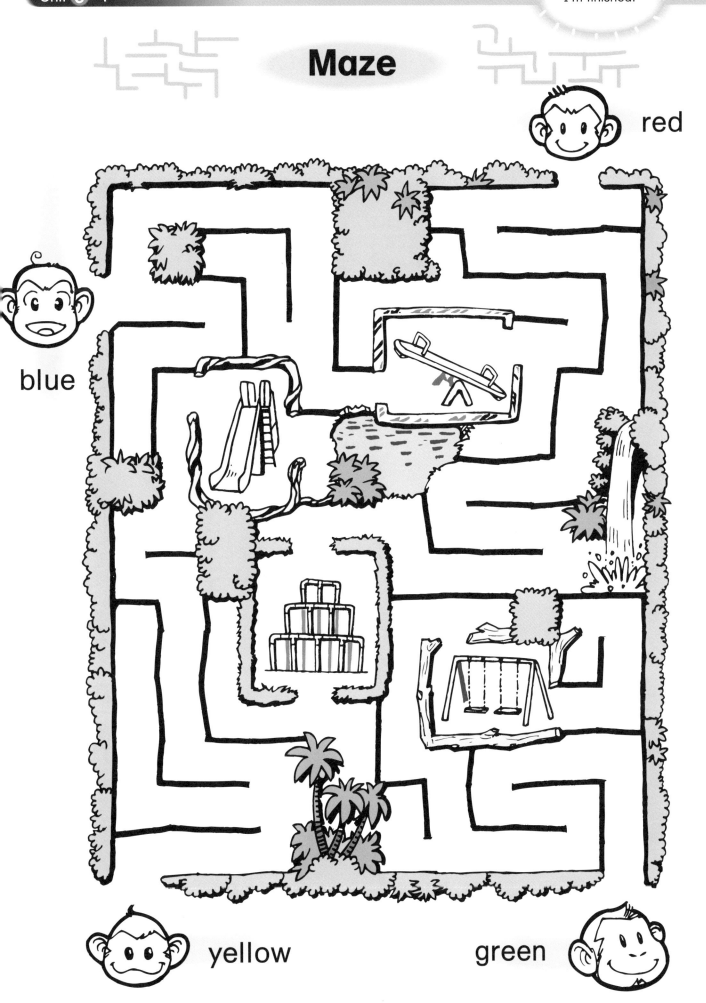

red

blue

yellow

green

How is the weather?

It is  today.

I like  days.

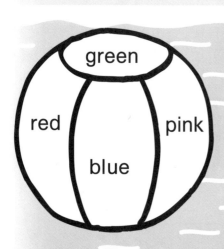
green
red | pink
blue

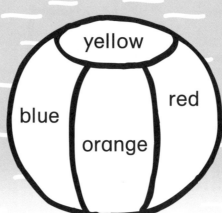
yellow
blue
orange
red

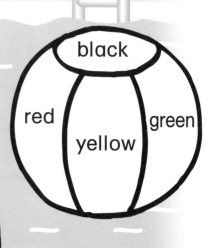
black
red | green
yellow

I'm finished!

up ↑ ↓ down

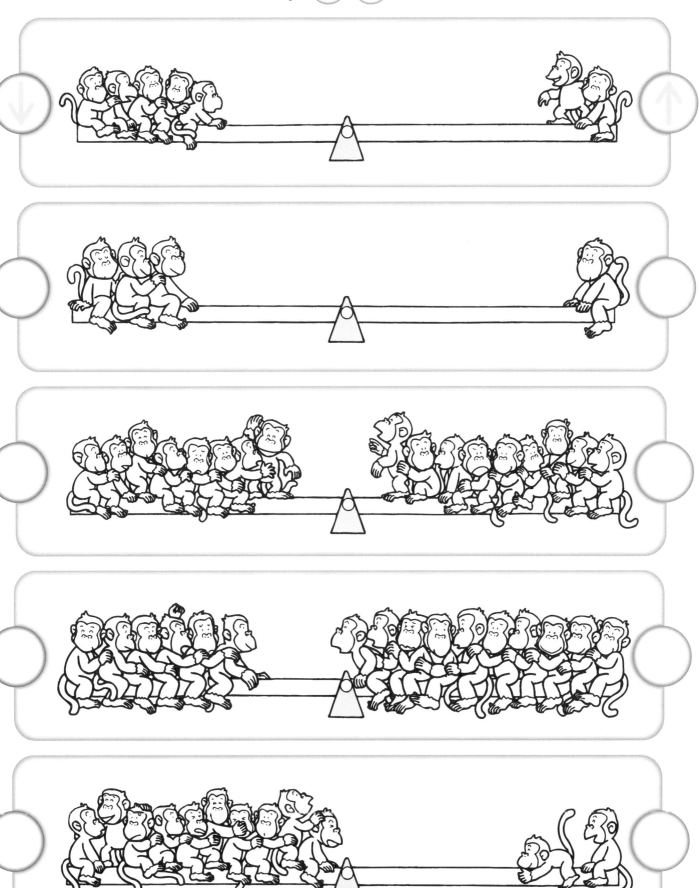

Number Bingo

1+2	1+1	2+2
1+0	2+3	3+3
6+3	4+3	5+3

2+5	5+4	2+1
3+1	4+3	3+2
5+5	1+1	4+4

2+4	1+3	0+1
1+6	1+1	4+1
3+6	6+2	3+7

2+0	1+2	3+1
6+1	3+5	2+4
1+9	4+1	6+3

上の4つのビンゴシートから1つを子供に選ばせてビンゴをしましょう。
Have each child choose a bingo board for each game.

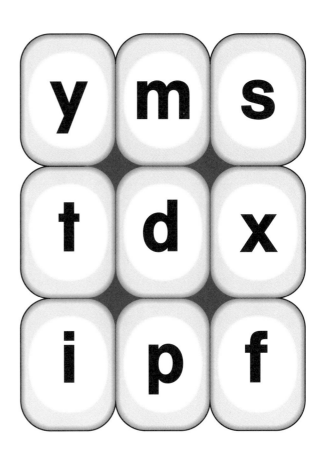

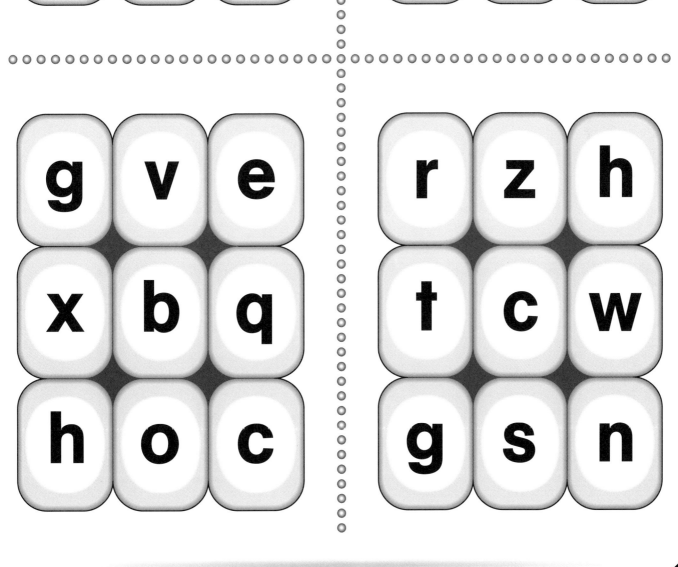

Action Bingo

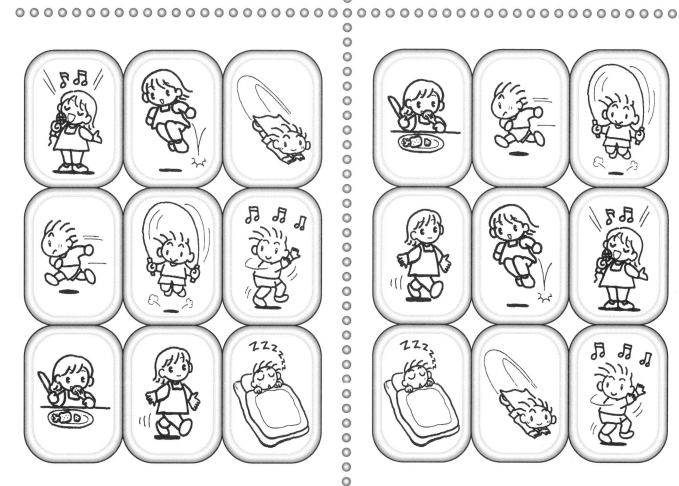